John Chick Murray

New England's Rural Winter

A poem

John Chick Murray

New England's Rural Winter
A poem

ISBN/EAN: 9783337254544

Printed in Europe, USA, Canada, Australia, Japan

Cover: Foto ©Thomas Meinert / pixelio.de

More available books at **www.hansebooks.com**

New England's Rural Winter:

A POEM.

BY

JOHN CHICK MURRAY.

WITH ILLUSTRATIONS.

NEW ENGLAND'S RURAL WINTER:

A POEM.

BY

JOHN CHICK MURRAY.

WITH ILLUSTRATIONS.

PORTLAND, MAINE:

TRANSCRIPT COMPANY.

1895.

New England's Rural Winter.

Thanksgiving Day once more has come and gone—
    That day to all our nation great and dear,
But in New England came whose earliest dawn,
    From night of persecution long and drear,
That night o'er foreign lands that hovered long,
    Its morning hours of peril o'er the wave,
Broke day at length upon a little throng,
    Who all its parts to God and freedom gave.

That day again, like hundreds of the past,
    Has raised the heart in gratitude and praise;
Once more our homes have made the yearly feast,
    And drawn their largest circle round the blaze:
Dear ones have met in childhood's sacred place,
    Long severed from those darling scenes apart;
The flush of youth once more has filled the face,
    And tender sighs and mem'ries filled the heart.

Now anxious cares have ceased to weigh the hour,
  Hearts, widowed long, have fled their lonely shade;
Old ties have gained a closer binding power,
  And here have been new loves and friendships made—
Now Winter's van has darkened o'er the leas,
  Migrating crows have lulled their clamorous strains;
The icy North has swayed the naked trees,
  And once again the bleak December reigns.

Now Phœbus, in his southern home retired,
  And driven there by heaven's eternal sway,
Shows not that glowing eye which lately fired
  The world, and lighted Summer's rosy way;
But through the chill and storm-preluding sky,
  How palely do his eye's far glances come!
As he beholds his daughter ravaged lie,
  And winter-woven cerements fold her form.

Chill over all New England's region spreads,
  In triumph fierce, the wintry conquest now;
O'er barren hills and mountains' bleaky heads,
  O'er dreary plains and sluggish vales below;
The river, erst fresh flowing, and the lake
  So shining, now are numbed in hoary death;
And does the leafless vegetation shake,
  O'er the dark heath, upon the angry breath.

4

Now overhead a sudden roar is heard,
    And groaning sound of heavy reeling trees;
And then alike are yonder regions stirred,
    By rushing gales, in merciless degrees;
Hark! now the fitful gusts, wild whirling, surge
    Against the doors, and at the windows rail,
Catching the smoke upon the chimney's verge,
    To hurl its thinning volume o'er the vale.

But Nature, in her leniency, recalls
    The actors of this boisterous theatre;
And when the evening's sable curtain falls,
    The tempest leaves the stage for action clear;
Now all is vacant, save when slumber's fays
    Steal in to occupy the silent scene,
And the mild stars await in vigil rays,
    The coming matinee to welcome in.

Thus till the streaky arms of coming Day,
    Reach forth and night's wide curtain slowly raise;
When are permitted on the stage to play,
    The gentle sunbeams for a day or days,
Till, darkly swarming in their northern hive,
    Rush forth the winds with sound of stormy war;
The flaky burdens now begin to drive,
    Increasing fast, and spreading wide and far.

See Nature, all her flaky hoard release,
　　Thick bleaching o'er the pinions of the storm,
So powdering winter's weather-tattered fleece,
　　When hurled upon his cold and sluggish form:
The ancient oak and elm are whitened o'er,
　　Seeming this hoary monster's scraggy horns;
And haply clogged the pecker's tiny door,
　　Appearing high upon the trunk or prongs.

The earth, late suffering from shocks and chills,
　　In virgin robes now deeply buried lies,
As Nature in regretful sorrow wills,
　　Like men, to show her kindness in demise:
Like men, who lavish on the needless dead,
　　Attention which they know will be the last;
And think they have those final moments made
　　To balance years of scorn and anger past.

But there is beauty even now, and hark!
　　The whistling northeast drives against the pane;
Day's hazy form is lost within the dark;
　　And Night wields o'er a hemisphere the reign:
With snow still heavy freighted is the blast,
　　That swiftly drives its slanting burdens down,
In crevices and corners sifting fast,
　　And raving rude the sober stantial round.

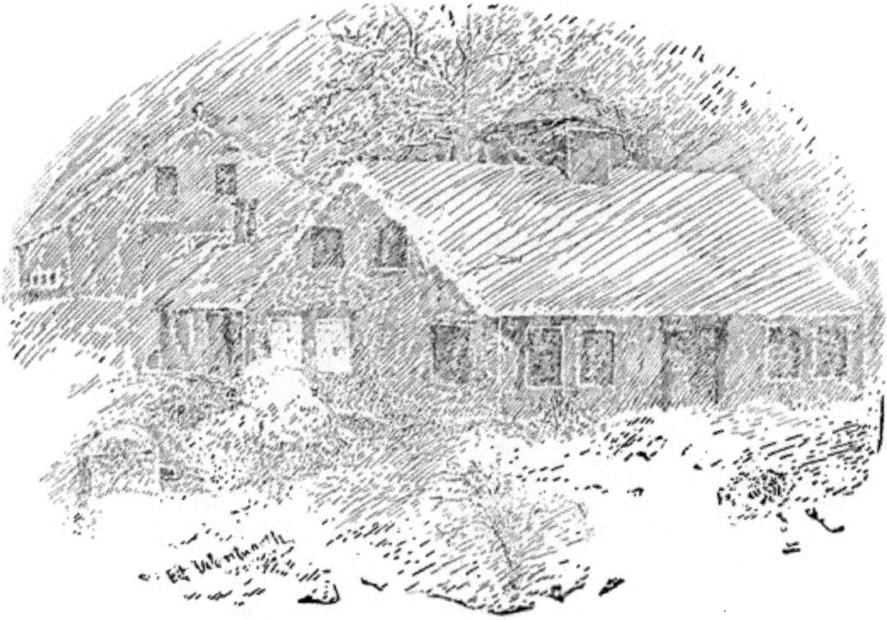

Woodpiles show dark and lonely mid the storm,
  And shortly sifted full and covered o'er;
And fast the drifts around the buildings form,
  And fill the naked bowers upon the moor.
Thus 'tis without, but let us look within:
  How like the nature of this human race;
When feeling hearts our graces often win,
  Though stormy frowns are rampant o'er the face!

Thus 'tis without, but let us look within:
  How snaps and roars the furnace well supplied!
How shows in front the briskly glowing scene,
  That warmly (unlike man) 'tis gratified!
How sweet the kettles bubble, sing and steam,
  As though they joyed o'er the preparing meal!
And on the shelf, the lamps how kingly seem!
  Whose bulging eyes affection seem to feel.

II

But how unlike the light of human eye!
  How free and full their glances shine around!
The painful presence of no enemy
  Can ever their all-reaching grace confound;
But kindly round the room, on old and young,
  They shed their cheering and impartial soul;
While human eyes all gloom and trouble shun,
  These sweetly on the raging tempest roll.

Yes, through the curtained and storm-pelted pane,
　　Athwart the gloom their lovely glances breast;
And on the Earth's unmitigated pain,
　　Freely their thousand twinkling sorrows rest;
And too, how often is their beamy light
　　The courier to 'nighted wand'rer's fear;
The golden pencils that impartial write
　　The hallowed words of home, and hope, and cheer!

Blow, blow, ye gales, and at the windows war;
　　Your raging only swells the beauty here;
Content, and happiness, and beauty, are
　　Within, and laughter takes the place of fear.
Glad are the youth to hear the storm go on;
　　And even now are planning divers ways
To utilize the virgin wealth at morn,
　　As we have all in by-gone happier days.

They talk of carving Winter's ghastly form,
　　From out the deeply pil'ed quarries white;
And how the statue can withstand the storm;
　　Which we all know will be their rapture's height:
Deeper the snow, the deeper be their bliss;
　　And happier they, the farther down they go;
Were we required to now accomplish this,
　　Ourselves would statues be of human snow.

The daughter's languaged eye and dimple's hue,
  Defy the tempest, and her silken hair
Waves only in the sighs of love that flow,
  In artless freedom, round her beauty fair;
And even grandma, in her corner warm,
  Begirt with children's prate and Pussy's " purr,"
With temples bleached in time's eternal storm,
  Her story tells, unmindful of the stir.

Affection fond and social beauty reign,
  By wholesome games and books diversified;
And still endeared by music's heavenly strain,
  Whose flow can stay the summer's ebbing tide;
As parents' eyes each offspring head survey,
  Their hearts with partial pride and fondness warm;
And night is turned into a cosy day;
  And sunny hearts dispel the cloud and storm.

III

Fled are the lovely birds of summer pride;
  Snow rudely clogs their lately verdant bowers;
Scattered their nests, their heaven-writ songs have died
  To waken only with the vernal flowers;
Save here and there some shiv'ring one remains,
  The last of summer's gay and dulcet choir,
Though but an echo of her former strains,
  A wand'ring cinder from her heavenly fire.

A tree anon wears yet a faded plume,
    Keen shiv'ring in the cruel winds alone--
Sad Autumn's garland left on Summer's tomb,
    Since parted long, and silent in her own.
As mourning yet their fated brothers slain,
    Above the snow some scattered sheaves appear--
Those keepsakes dear my bosom would retain,
    As sacred locks from Autumn's yellow hair.

The owl, with loneliness her mate serene,
    Passes in dumb and dreamy mood the day;
But when her starry auditors convene,
    And Evening hangs her sable scenery,
On some old tree, its grandeur in the wane,
    That lonely looks across the wintry night,
In all the volume of her mournful strain,
    She blends her woe with setting Luna's light.

The partridge, startled from her secret bower,
    On whirring pinion her intruder flies,
But crash! the bursting flame and leaden shower,
    Her plumage drench, and tear her vital ties.
The cunning fox is bounding for his lair,
    And savagely by yelling hounds pursued;
But spite of all his speed and crafty care,
    His calm is ransomed only with his blood.

And 'long his narrow, thicket-piercing road,
    Gay runs the innocent and timid hare;
E'en he, to satisfy the thirst for blood,
    Falls by the gory shot or cruel snare.
And thus the timid and the shrewd alike,
    The innocent, the guilty and the brave,
Must fall to fill man's barbarous delight,—
    Think! our delight a happy creature's grave!

So fate is wonted everywhere below:
    Man's cruel aims some victim ever find;
Or innocent or guilty, friend or foe,
    His heart is ever the destroying kind.
Revenge pursues a fleeing brother's breath,
    While in ambition's race a thousand fall;
Cold Envy plans our reputation's death,
    And pampered passion bleeds the peace of all.

The axe is busy in its silvern home,
    The glaring slayer of its shelt'ring tree;
Whose measured notes, far sounding, sweetly form
    A happy scale of rural industry.
Along the field and winding woodland ways,
    Moves slowly Fuel's car—of future bright;
The faithful steer seems conscious he conveys
    The coming chief of many a happy night.

Far in the field or by the way appears
    That sacred mark upon the map of earth:
The roomy house, the style of former years;
    The shelter where our fathers had their birth;
Nay, neath its roof New England's self was born;
    Here Freedom rocked her infancy to rest;
The cheeks that blossomed here her grace adorn;
    And love, here nourished, warms her hilly breast.

Within, content and happiness repose,
    And doubled from the cellar's treasured worth,
Jack Frost avoiding through the cuddling snows,
    Which very robes he wore from the far north:
Here is preserved the blood of Summer warm,
    And closed 'neath Autumn's sure and ripening seal;
Though buried be her torn and faded form,
    The family scenes her cheering spirit feel.

The Fire-king, so luxuriant and bright,
    'Gainst winter bravely bears his flaming shield;
Though chill and tempest wage determined fight,
    They're driven from the kitchen's cosy field;
And Summer's spirit fosters in his care;
    He, for her safety, bares his glaring breast;
And in the face of winter's haughty air,
    His smoking rage blows from the chimney's crest.

Oh! were the fire upon this fleshly hearth,
    That passion fire thus true, and never false;
The freezing storms of sorrow driving forth,
    Its gracious office ever to repulse;
To dry away the lingering tear of grief;
    To melt the ice of want to plenty's flame;
Upon the slandered name some brightness leave,
    And kindle hope within the heart of shame.

Hark! list that world-involving tone of bells,
    Sweet ushering in the merry Christmas tide,
Which over our snow-lighted hills and dells,
    Awake a sense of happiness and pride;
This festal hour with joy and laurel teems!
    Flows everywhere the tide of rich acclaim;
This earth-wide scene of celebration seems
    The vestry 'neath Heaven's auditorium.

The world is gathered in these lower halls,
    In choral joy and ceremonial plan,
By heart impelled or custom's firmer calls,
    To honor Him who lived and died for man;
To praise in love and veneration due,
    That hour when earth a friend and teacher found
A hero to his lofty mission true.
    Yet, with his glory, shed his blood around.

Ye myriads who profusely serve the time,
  Gay in rejoicing met and music free,
(Mid Christmas lights) whose bright affection's clime
  Blooms rich in tokens on the laded " tree;"
Pause once amid your sparkling merriment,
  To list the still small whispers that arise,
And make your own a birth of glad event,
  And everything to duty sacrifice.

And further this divinest lesson mind,
  Which we should mould each aim and action by—
To think and throb, to suffer for mankind,
  And, if required, for truth and man to die:
Nor wavering pause to think your fate severe;
  Oft does the world such retribution make;
So soothes the pang, the wearied brain and tear,
  Of those who dare and labor for her sake.

Ye now enquire whence life's unfailing meed,
  Or where th' incentive lies to persevere,
Or what it boots the heart or veins to bleed,
  If such attend and close our efforts here;
Know this, our purest joy is duty done;
  Its consciousness the toil and tear will pay;
Beside, the noble work, though now unsung,
  Will grace our dust, and bless the world some day.

'Tis market day; the lusty prancer plays,
    The fondled youngster of some "standard-bred;"
Which noble bloods our horses often grace,
    And honor on New England horsemen shed;
Or it may be the grandsire's aged friend,
    And faithful servant of his better year;
And still together they the hill descend;
    And each, far backward, sees his prime uprear.

And from the harvest's ample treasury,
    Amounts are gathered of intrinsic worth,
And roundly piled the market to supply,
    Fresh, unadulterate from mother earth:
The field and garden treasures pouring forth,
    Give honor to their pioneer, the plow;
The dairy contributes it's yellow worth,
    And casts a gold reflection on the cow.

Nor should the cow receive the praise alone,
    The earth-subduing plow and Nature's grace,—
The Sun, that in his growing glory shone,
    And rain, that laved the earth's enfevered face;
But in this 'cumulated wealth appears
    The gathered labor of the mother's hands,
The father's husbandry and faithful cares,—
    'Tis God and man together till the lands.

So in the agriculture of the heart,
    Thought's warming sun and feeling's tearful rain,
May faithfully perform their wonted part,
    But Resolution's self must till the plain;
And when she toils with energy and will,
    What crops of goodness spring from all the ground!
What flowers of happiness the gardens fill!
    What fields of friendship flourish all around!

And every day some worthy care assigns;
    And care that lofty place in honor holds;
That on the hearth of evening nobly shines,
    And in the welfare of the barns and folds.
Thus, independent, with a quiet chance
    For rest, the farmer's winter flies away,
Till some fair morning gives a sunny glance,
    That he is wanted in the woods that day.

But quickly flies the day, by nature short,
    And by his happiness made shorter still;
And evening calls him from his genial work,
    To scenes that make all human fathers thrill:
His light and fire a cheering spirit lend,
    And all around in guilding beauty fall.
A world's wide limits everywhere extend,
    But yet this little spot is worth them all.

Though fancy far on truant wing may soar,
  And cull the pride a thousand climes impart,
And e'en the heavenly circles may explore,
  This little circle ever holds the heart.
And mark the welcome which attends him here—
  Welcome that otherwhere he never found;
Though traversed earth's wide limits far and near,
  'Tis home alone that speaks the welcome sound.

His happy group familiar press around,
  The dearest portions of his blood and heart;
The mother's cares in all the scene abound;
  She binds the whole, and yet she fills each part:
Mid such a scene appears the supper board,
  By wife or daughter's ready labor graced;
And, largely from the cellar's wealthy hoard,
  The home enjoys what's better than a feast.

This makes him prize the ever-willing steer,
  And Independence's vehicle, the plow;
And when the butter and the milk appear,
  He proudly feels the value of the cow:
With plenty thus his evening board supplied,
  The heart as amply with affection's glow,
The long cold evenings of the winter glide
  With beauty which our farmers only know.

Though sparkling frost may gem Night's coronet,
  Here in her heart are glowing love and fire;
Here are that beauty, worth and honor met,
  New England has, and all the world admire;
And from the scene that here serenely beams,
  Oft Genius culls her bright and native spark;
From noble lore and earth's illustrious names,
  Ambition kindles in some head and heart.

And to these fires our worth is largely traced,
  In many noble sons around them bred;
Whose efforts have their country's welfare graced,
  And on the world a pride and blessing shed:
Here statesmanship has found its dawning light;
  Here eloquence its spark of thrilling fire;
Here valor sprang to guard the Nation's right;
  And here has inspiration strung the lyre.

Thus, as our mountain streams, obscure and lone,
  Swell into manufacture's vital veins;
Or, as our twigs to spars and masts are grown,
  To bear our products o'er the ocean plains;
So do our sons on native hillsides, cast
  Their genius till are glory's spindles whirled;
Or genius' twig becomes a mighty mast,
  To waft our worth and honor round the world.

Nor can these daughters be refused our pride,
　　Whose bosoms are the fertile vales of all;
Whose tender influence rolls a stronger tide
　　Than ocean, held in Luna's heavenly thrall;
For only twice a month can Luna heap
　　The wave along the counter-braving shore;
But this fair Luna ever swells the deep
　　Of human life, all earth and ocean o'er.

And every virtue which the lyre has rung,
　　Was nourished in her lovely womanhood;
And every ill that round the cradle hung,
　　Was soothed or banished by her fortitude.
Too proudly can our grateful bosoms prize
　　The sisters, wives and mothers of to-day;
The sisters, wives and mothers in the skies;
　　The sisters, wives and mothers yet to be?

IX

Now from these vital scenes we turn without,
　　To other charms the wintry hours present:
The winds are blowing, and the stars are out,
　　Cold twinkling from the sable firmament:
The Northern lights in shifting brightness show,
　　Which brightness though shows not the cause of it;
Haply the skating-fire of Esquimaux,
　　Or it may be the flashes of their wit.

The cold and rain have joined their properties,
    And on the ponds a sheeny splendor laid;
The lusty youth have summoned their allies,
    And hither have their noisy errands made.
Lo! now the snapping bonfire, rich and fierce
    Upflaring, throws its light and warmth around;
And o'er the cracking and loud rumbling ice,
    The boisterous shout and clatt'ring skates resound.

And oft our girls are sprinkled in the crowd,
    (And temper rudeness with their beauty sweet)
For what avails the wind, or cold, or cloud,
    When in the country youth and pleasure meet?
The heart of youth is nature's boiling-spring,
    Impelling high its heated blood and round;
Its sparkling spray sweet colors everything,
    With colors though which often do confound.

Some farmer's house, full lighted, sweetly throws
    Inviting glances from its window eyes—
Such eyes as shine beneath New England's brows,
    And speak the heart wherein her grandeur lies:
And how these kindly invitations call,
    And cheering urge the neighbors on their way,
Till 'neath his roof are gaily gathered all,
    To share an evening's hospitality!

Kindly and free the neighboring homes convene;
    And though the while the vacant house be dark,
Each home, from this bright home-uniting scene,
    Will carry back a new and brighter spark.
So should the heart, when social love invite,
    Close up and leave her lonely house and drear;
Rake up the fire, blow out the feeble light,
    And in some other bosom find a cheer.

Or haply now the District School House swells,
    Into the heart of night, its shining floods,
While laughing groups and merry chiming bells,
    Are slowly nearing on the distant roads;
Behold the choosers take their wonted nook,
And note their shrewd and anxious choosing calls;
    Then see the master glean the spelling book,
And pass the products 'round the crowded walls.

Or the defaced and ancient walls may ring
    (Walls ever fair and sacred to us all,
While yet our hearts, refreshed from childhood's spring.
    The dawning time and careless hour recall),
From the loud chorus of the country round,
    Directed by the singing-master's care;
Or may these walls in reverent awe resound
    With accents of the country pastor's prayer.

That district School House! sacred is its form!
    The cradle of New England culture keen,
Rocked in th' invigorating wind and storm,
    As since, the hearts that labored there have been!
Recline not o'er its surplus benches now
    The motley throng that gathered here of yore,
When, harvest done, and silent was the plow,
    Our fathers came to share its wholesome lore.

Of learning may more gorgeous systems shine
    And shame the School House from its parent hill,
(The Alma Mater that is dearly mine;
    And where I felt the first aspiring thrill)
Unshaken still, its influence remains,
    Based on that hardly worth it helped to rear;
The light reflected from its scanty panes
    Came fresh from heaven, and is immortal here.

Oh! let my breast a longer season thrill,
    As to my thought one treasured roof appears!
Oh! let my soul once more that structure fill,
    And hang the garlands of my love and tears!
Faces and forms I there espy of old;
    Nor in the garments wove by time and care;
Nor in the cerements of the crumbling mould;
    But as I saw their youth and beauty there.

And, ere I can th' impatient theme resume,
    One other school room brightens in my breast,
Where, from her long recess within the tomb,
    One darling form is to my bosom pressed.
Sweet angel! thy immortal part has shone
    Long in my breast, and now corrosive Death
Seems yielding all he ever called his own,
    Fresh blooming in thy bosom-heaving breath.

Still down thy neck that tress of raven hue
    Hangs like the parted cloud o'er heaven's brow,
Through which would oft my youthful fancy view
    Thine eyes as suns, that shine upon me now:
Like zephyrs on New England's flowery hills,
    Still on thy lips abound those gentle sighs;
That ruddy hue thy cheek of beauty fills,
    Like rising day upon the early skies.

Lo! this is Saturday's descending sun;
    And home is with anticipation bright,
Turned fondly toward some dear and absent one,
    Who from his toil and care returns to-night.
How welcome is thy parting, Sun of time,
    Where at thy set another son will come;
Or when the daughter's bosom-shining clime,
    Thy setting brings, in weekly brightness home.

Sweet home! the casket of the human breast,
    Where feeling's sweetest smiles and tears are lain;
Where all our dearest hopes and mem'ries rest,
    And all the surest remedies for pain.
Completed is the tender circle now,
    Dissevered lately by some neighb'ring town;
A brighter light is shown upon each brow—
    A light reflected never from a crown.

The hearth is now in extra measure fed;
    The table tidier and more fully dressed;
The well-trimmed lamps a brighter lustre shed;
    To cheer and welcome home the kindred guest;
The children haste the happ'nings to convey,
    Or take some present for their joy designed;
The faithful dog shows gladness in his way,
    And Puss is pleased another lap to find.

The home a full and shining circle show.
    Save in some part a wand'ring shadow lay,
Where Death broke in the circle long ago,
    And bore a darling from the scene away:
In yonder yard, where winters vainly rave,
    Some form, once lighting here, now wasting lies;
Whose smiles and tears are frozen in the grave,
    Forever paled whose home-illuming eyes.

But memory unbars the frozen tomb,
    And, like the life, refills the vacant chair;
Kindly restores each death-imprisoned bloom
    And wakes again the silent voices there;
While the fond spirit, life and light of all,
    Lives in her prestige, 'bove the Spoiler's power;
Her deathless smile upon each heart will fall
    And light this home unto its latest hour.

The gentle hours of evening onward flow,
    And happily they pass the week's decline,
With hearth yet warm, and lamps that brightly glow,
    Till now their beams o'er midnight's valley shine;
When all the members hie them to repose;
    Full shortly is the chamber drap'ry drawn;
Now kindly sleep does Nature's curtains close
    And softly nurse her till the tardy morn.

Such is the slumber vagrants fain would prove;
    Such is the slumber monarchs vainly crave;
Though loud the cold is cracking in the roof,
    And loud the winds around the windows rave:
No sounding pavements ruffle the repose;
    No riot fears the pillow's calm profane,
But smoothly on the stream of slumber flows
    Until it floods the morning's shiny plain.

'Tis Sabbath now, and Morn, with glowing soul,
    Stands gracious on his heavenly altar grand;
Seems, in his spreading lustre, to unroll
    Devotion's halcyon programme o'er the land:
A thousand temples lift their spiry crowns,
    To catch the tone of heavenly symphony;
Then their deep voices pour their pealing sounds
    The mighty organ of the world to-day.

And from their choir, which all New England fills,
    Their iron tongues the voluntary peal:
Lo! see it waken all our vales and hills,
    And bid the soul an inspiration feel.
Our homes, responsive to the summons wide,
    Largely devotion's pious walks attend;
Or, consecrating home and fireside,
    To God upon the heart's own altar bend.

And piety's true altar is the heart;
    And every holy thought must worship there;
And in that humble and aspiring part,
    Must offer its divinist psalm and prayer.
There conscience, God's apostle, ever stands,
    And from His volume teaches the divine,—
Nor circumscribed, but in all human lands,
    And in all times, his heavenly sermons shine.

Such is the land I proudly call my own;
  Such is the soil my yearly furrows tear;
Such are the scenes, to other lands unknown,
  'Mong which are passed my joy, and pain, and care;
Such are the hills whereon I thrill and glow,
  As I afar these rural homes survey;
Such are the hearths that warm my bosom so,
  And light the friends and places dear to me.

Such are the hearths whose cheer-awaking flame
  Flashes upon one darling face the glow,
And brightens round one ever-haunting name,
  That fills my soul with beauty, love and woe;
With beauty to behold that Heavenly art
  So richly o'er her form and features shine;
With love to feel the beauty of her heart;
  With pain to know they never can be mine.

Such are the skies that bended o'er my birth,
  And such will see my fate or fortune passed;
And kindly will our rock-ennobled earth
  Unfold and wrap these weary bones at last.
How enviable the quiet in such ground!
  Where slumber they from whom our annals rose;
Though I, like them, shall never sleep renowned,
  'Twere sweet to vie with them but in repose.

Such sturdy scenes New England's glory make,
 Her poems, too, when pencils peer the theme;
Scenes ever which the noblest rapture wake,
 And proudly merit genius' brightest beam;
Such are the scenes that wake this holy fire
 Within my heart of beauty, love and pride,
Wherein is fondly flaming this desire,
 (A prouder goal than all the world beside.)

To raise my lyre in grandeur to my theme,
 To fill my verse as passion fills my veins,
And leave at last another worthy name,
 And fit memorial to my native plains.
With her my prayer through all her onward race,
 My pride and love deep rooted in her sod,
I leave New England in her Sabbath grace,
 Grand in her homes, her annals and her God.

North Berwick, Me., Nov. 5, 1895,

www.ingramcontent.com/pod-product-compliance
Lightning Source LLC
Chambersburg PA
CBHW021456090426
42739CB00009B/1752